Effective Classroom Assessment:

Linking Assessment with Instruction

Catherine Garrison

Dennis Chandler

Michael Ehringhaus

National Middle School Association and Measured Progress

Westerville, Ohio

National Middle School Association
www.nmsa.org

Measured Progress
www.measuredprogress.org

Library of Congress Cataloging-in-Publication Data

Garrison, Catherine, date.
Effective classroom assessment : linking assessment with instruction / Measured Progress Professional Development Group, Catherine Garrison, Dennis Chandler, and Michael Ehringhaus.
    p. cm. -- (A professional development resource for schools or teams)
Includes bibliographical references and index.
ISBN 978-1-56090-228-7 (alk. paper)
1. Educational tests and measurements--United States. 2. Middle school students--Rating of--United States. 3. Middle school education--United States--Standards. 4. Educational accountability--United States. 5. Effective teaching--United States.
I. Chandler, Dennis, date. II. Ehringhaus, Michael, date. III. Measured Progress Professional Development Group. IV. Title.
LB3060.26.G36 2009
373.126′4--dc22
                    2009009468

Contents

Getting Started

Assessment has always been an integral component of education, but the stakes have changed. For decades, one of the primary purposes of the assessments used by districts and schools was to rank order students to assist in tracking them into either a college preparatory program or a vocational training program. Now, every state due to *No Child Left Behind* has the challenge of ensuring that "all students will and can learn." States are held accountable, through adequate yearly progress, for demonstrating that this goal is achieved. All educators are now responsible for evaluating student progress in terms of mastery of standards designed by each state to prepare students for 21st century skills. Standards are the skills and knowledge that students need to know at different points in their academic careers. The statewide accountability assessments are aligned to these standards.

The movement toward standards-based assessment has led to a major paradigm shift in the way educators plan, instruct, and evaluate their students. All aspects of curriculum, instruction, and assessment must be aligned to a series of standards. This is often a challenge for both veteran teachers who have been in the classrooms for years and for new teachers just beginning their careers. For many, the emphasis on accountability has led to a more stressful environment where it seems all energies are targeted at statewide assessments. These changes have left many students and parents, as well as teachers, confused and uncertain about the intended objectives and exactly what students are to know and be able to do.

Over the past few years, educational research has targeted the most effective ways to improve student achievement. One significant area of research is in effective classroom assessment practices. Effective classroom assessment happens when educators understand the importance of using high-quality assessments during all phases of learning; this is referred to as one aspect of Assessment Literacy. Student achievement improves when assessment is seen as both an instructional tool during the learning process as well as an accountability tool to determine if learning has occurred (Stiggins, 2003).

Educators must practice the attributes of assessment literacy by gathering dependable information about student achievement, using various assessment methods, and interpreting the results to promote and encourage student growth. Teachers should use formative assessment to gather information about individual students during the learning process and use this information to guide and adjust instruction. Teachers also should use summative assessments for accountability and to demonstrate where students are at a particular point in time in regard to specific knowledge and skills.

In middle school practice, this shift in assessment thinking intersects with National Middle School Association's research summary *Characteristics of Exemplary Schools for Young Adolescents* (2006). In this summary, assessment is defined as the information-gathering process that creates a conduit for feedback about student understanding. Ongoing assessment during the instructional process informs teachers and students and provides a means for identifying gaps and misconceptions, allowing for appropriate and immediate interventions. For students, the feedback from teachers or peers creates a culture in which assessment becomes a tool to guide them in metacognitive reflection about their learning in relation to intended expectations. This assessment process places students at the center of their own learning and success. A student-centered classroom approach is essential to exemplary practice in middle level education.

Research has proven that when classroom assessment practices, both summative and formative, are implemented effectively, the students showing the greatest gains are those who typically perform at the lower level of achievement measures (Black & Wiliam, 1998). Effective assessment practices actually close learning gaps. Furthermore, effective classroom assessment practices not only require educators to be assessment literate, they also place more responsibility for learning on the individual student. Engaged students take ownership of their learning and become the center of their own success. When the classroom culture becomes one of support and encouragement, students are more likely to take risks and expand their own learning. When the instructional relationship between student and teacher tightens, the goal of maximizing student learning is more likely to be realized.

An Overview of the Content

This resource contains readings, materials, and activities designed to engage teams of teachers in self-reflection and discussions about their current assessment practices. The goal of this experience is for teachers to come away with an understanding of the value of linking their assessment practices with their classroom instructional practices. Each of the modules includes background information about its content, activities, and tasks. The modules are designed to engage participants in reflection on their current instructional practices and to encourage discussions with peers about effective ways of improving their classroom assessment practices. Each of the modules has a primary focus supported by research and provides links to published articles and references to other related publications. This publication is ultimately a blueprint for a professional inquiry process that enables individuals and teams of educators to learn about effective classroom assessment, to reflect on current practices, and to discuss their own findings and their own discovered ways to improve assessment practices.

Module I—Assessment, Standards, and Targets:

Part 1 provides a basic understanding of assessment and the distinct characteristics of summative and formative assessment. Part 2 looks at the relationship between standards, curriculum, instruction, and assessment. The tasks help to deepen the understanding of assessment and the role of standards and targets in the classroom.

Module II—Assessment Methods and Item Design:

Part 1 shares information about the variety of assessments that are available and their appropriate uses. Part 2 discusses item design— i.e., the construction of an item. The tasks demonstrate the value of different assessment methods and the importance of good item construction.

Module III—Instructional Assessment in the Classroom:

Part 1 provides an understanding of formative assessment as an instructional practice. Part 2 describes the importance of multiple data-gathering sources. Part 3 presents the essential strategy of descriptive feedback. The tasks expand understanding of formative assessment so that teachers can effectively introduce them into their own classroom practices.

While there are a number of ways the materials can be used, we suggest using small, facilitated study groups or teams followed by cross-team faculty discussions. This approach encourages educators to share their findings and reflections regarding good assessment practice. Involving colleagues in these discussions of effective classroom practices is a supportive way to grow as a professional learning community focused on improving student learning.

"For teachers to be successful in constructing new roles, they need opportunities to participate in a professional community that discusses new teacher materials and strategies and that supports the risk-taking and struggle entailed in transforming practice" (Putnam & Borko, 2000).

Module I
Assessment, Standards, and Targets

Part 1—What Is Assessment?

What is assessment? Assessment is the process of collecting information. In the classroom, it is the gathering of evidence of student learning and a tool that informs and encourages student growth. What constitutes effective classroom assessment? Effective assessment provides evidence of student performance relative to content and performance standards. It provides teachers and students with insight into student errors and misconceptions and helps lead the teacher directly to action. As educators, we should strive to create and maintain effective classroom assessment practices, including both high-quality formative measures and summative assessments.

There is a wide variety of assessments used effectively in the classroom, ranging from a pencil-and-paper quiz to the creation of a product or performance of a skill. The assessments may simply allow students to recall basic information, or they may expect students to combine the elements and parts of several standards, skills, or concepts to make more complex judgments. These will be discussed in further detail in Module II.

Activity—Formative and Summative Assessment in the Classroom: Read and React

Directions: After each member of the team has read the article *Formative and Summative Assessment in the Classroom*, complete each of the tasks identified.

Formative and Summative Assessments in the Classroom
Catherine Garrison and Michael Ehringhaus, Ph.D.

Successful middle schools engage students in all aspects of their learning. There are many strategies for accomplishing this. One such strategy is student-led conferences. As a classroom teacher or administrator, how do you ensure that the information shared in a student-led conference provides a balanced picture of the student's strengths and weaknesses? The answer to this is to balance both summative and formative classroom assessment practices and information gathering about student learning.

Assessment is a huge topic that encompasses everything from statewide accountability tests to district benchmark or interim tests to everyday classroom tests. In order to grapple with what seems to be an overuse of testing, educators should frame their views of testing as assessment and that assessment is information. The more information we have about students, the clearer the picture we have about achievement or where gaps may occur.

Defining Formative and Summative Assessments
The terms "formative" and "summative" do not have to be difficult, yet the definitions have become confusing in the past few years. This is especially true for formative assessment. In a balanced assessment system, both summative and formative assessments are an integral part of information gathering. Depend too much on one or the other and the reality of student achievement in your classroom becomes unclear.

Summative Assessments are given periodically to determine at a particular point in time what students know and do not know. Many associate summative assessments only with standardized tests such as state assessments, but they are also used at and are an important part of district and classroom programs. Summative assessment at the district and classroom level is an accountability measure that is generally used as part of the grading process. The list is long, but here are some examples of summative assessments:

- State assessments

- District benchmark or interim assessments

- End-of-unit or chapter tests

- End-of-term or semester exams

- Scores that are used for accountability of schools (AYP) and students (report card grades).

The key is to think of summative assessment as a means to gauge, at a particular point in time, student learning relative to content standards. Although the information gleaned from this type of assessment is important, it can only help in evaluating certain aspects of the learning process. Because they are spread out and occur after instruction every few weeks, months, or once a year, summative assessments are tools to help evaluate the effectiveness of programs, school improvement goals, alignment of curriculum, or student placement in specific programs. Summative assessments happen too far down the learning path to provide information at the classroom level and to make instructional adjustments and interventions *during* the learning process. It takes formative assessment to accomplish this.

Formative Assessment is part of the instructional process. When incorporated into classroom practice, it provides the information needed to adjust teaching and learning while they are happening. In this sense, formative assessment informs both teachers and students about student understanding at a point when timely adjustments can be made. These adjustments help to ensure students achieve targeted standards-based learning goals within a set time frame. Although formative assessment strategies appear in a variety of formats, there are some distinct ways to distinguish them from summative assessments.

One distinction is to think of formative assessment as "practice." We do not hold students accountable in "grade book fashion" for skills and concepts they have just been introduced to or are learning. We must allow for practice. Formative assessment helps teachers determine next steps during the learning process as the instruction approaches the summative assessment of student learning. A good analogy for this is the road test that is required to receive a driver's license. What if, before getting your driver's license, you received a grade every time you sat behind the wheel to practice driving? What if your final grade for the driving test was the average of all of the grades you received while practicing? Because of the initial low grades you received during the process of learning to drive, your final grade would not accurately reflect your ability to drive a car. In the beginning of learning to drive, how confident or motivated to learn would you feel? Would any of the grades you received provide you with guidance on what you needed to do next to improve your driving skills? Your final driving test, or summative assessment, would be the accountability measure that establishes whether or not you have the driving skills necessary for a driver's license—not a reflection of all the driving practice that leads to it. The same holds true for classroom instruction, learning, and assessment.

Another distinction that underpins formative assessment is student involvement. If students are not involved in the assessment process, formative assessment is not practiced or implemented to its full effectiveness. Students need to be involved both as assessors of their own learning and as resources to other students. There are numerous strategies teachers can implement to engage students. In fact, research shows that the involvement in and ownership of their work increases students' motivation to learn. This does not mean the absence of teacher involvement. To the contrary, teachers are critical in identifying learning goals, setting clear criteria for success, and designing assessment tasks that provide evidence of student learning.

One of the key components of engaging students in the assessment of their own learning is providing them with descriptive feedback as they learn. In fact, research shows descriptive feedback to be the most significant instructional strategy to move students forward in their learning. Descriptive feedback provides students with an understanding of what they are doing well, links to classroom learning, and gives specific input on how to reach the next step in the learning progression. In other words, descriptive feedback is not a grade, a sticker, or "good job!" A significant body of research indicates that such limited feedback does not lead to improved student learning.

There are many classroom instructional strategies that are part of the repertoire of good teaching. When teachers use sound instructional practice for the purpose of gathering information on student learning, they are applying this information in a formative way. In this sense, formative assessment is pedagogy and clearly cannot be separated from instruction. It is what good teachers do. The distinction lies in what teachers actually do with the information they gather. How is it being used to inform instruction? How is it being shared with and engaging students? It's not teachers just collecting information/data on student learning; it's what they do with the information they collect.

Some of the instructional strategies that can be used formatively include the following:

Criteria and goal setting with students engages them in instruction and the learning process by creating clear expectations. In order to be successful, students need to understand and know the learning target/goal and the criteria for reaching it. Establishing and defining quality work together, asking students to participate in establishing norm behaviors for classroom culture, and determining what should be included in criteria for success are all examples of this strategy. Using student work, classroom tests, or exemplars of what is expected helps students understand where they are, where they need to be, and an effective process for getting there.

Observations go beyond walking around the room to see if students are on task or need clarification. Observations assist teachers in gathering evidence of student learning to inform instructional planning. This evidence can be recorded and used as feedback for students about their learning or as anecdotal data shared with them during conferences.

Questioning strategies should be embedded in lesson/unit planning. Asking better questions allows an opportunity for deeper thinking and provides teachers with significant insight into the degree and depth of understanding. Questions of this nature engage students in classroom dialogue that both uncovers and expands learning. An "exit slip" at the end of a class period to determine students' understanding of the day's lesson or quick checks during instruction such as "thumbs up/down" or "red/green" (stop/go) cards are also examples of questioning strategies that elicit immediate information about student learning. Helping students ask better questions is another aspect of this formative assessment strategy.

Self and peer assessment helps to create a learning community within a classroom. Students who can reflect while engaged in metacognitive thinking are involved in their learning. When students have been involved in criteria and goal setting, self-evaluation is a logical step in the learning process. With peer evaluation, students see each other as resources for understanding and checking for quality work against previously established criteria.

Student record keeping helps students better understand their own learning as evidenced by their classroom work. This process of students keeping ongoing records of their work not only engages students, it also helps them, beyond a "grade," to see where they started and the progress they are making toward the learning goal.

All of these strategies are integral to the formative assessment process, and they have been suggested by models of effective middle school instruction.

Balancing Assessment

As teachers gather information/data about student learning, several categories may be included. In order to better understand student learning, teachers need to consider information about the products (paper or otherwise) students create and tests they take, observational notes, and reflections on the communication that occurs between teacher and student or among students. When a comprehensive assessment program at the classroom level balances formative and summative student learning/achievement information, a clear picture emerges of where a student is relative to learning targets and standards. Students should be able to articulate this shared information about their own learning. When this happens, student-led conferences, a formative assessment strategy, are valid. The more we know about individual students as they engage in the learning process, the better we can adjust instruction to ensure that all students continue to achieve by moving forward in their learning.

References

Black, P., Harrison, C., Lee, C., Marshall, B., & Wiliam, D. (2003) *Assessment for Learning: Putting it into practice.* Berkshire, England: Open University Press.

Butler, D.L. & Winnie, P.H. (1995) Feedback and self-regulated learning: a theoretical synthesis. *Review of Educational Research, 65*(3), 245-281.

Sadler, D.R. (1998) Formative assessment: revisiting the territory. *Assessment in Education, 5*(1), 77-84.

Task One: Use the reading to frame your thinking about your current understanding and your practices of classroom assessment, e.g., what I have learned, what I practice, and how I could improve. Meet with your team and complete the *Assessment Characteristics T-Chart* below. List the characteristics of formative and summative assessments, providing rationale for each. Remember, it's not the assessment itself that necessarily categorizes it as either formative or summative; it's the use and purpose of the assessment.

Assessment Characteristics T-Chart

Formative Assessment	Summative Assessment

Task Two: What types of assessment do you use in your classroom? Use the *Current Classroom Assessment Practices Survey* below to track your assessments over several weeks.

Current Classroom Assessment Practices Survey

Please use this template as a guide to record your assessment practices over a period of time. You may reproduce this template as necessary for the amount of space needed.

Pre-Instructional Assessments

Description of Pre-Assessment	DOK or Bloom Level	Standards Addressed

Assessments during the Instructional/Learning Process—Formative

Description of Formative Assessment	How often or when is this technique used?	How is information used?

Post-Instructional Assessments—Summative

Descriptionof Summative Assessment	DOK or Bloom Level	Standards Addressed

1. How are students involved in their own assessment?

2. How are students involved in assessing themselves?

3. How are students involved with peer assessment or as resources for each other?

4. How do you use descriptive feedback to engage students and to move them forward in their learning?

5. What assessment accommodations or adaptations do you use for various students?

Provide any other information regarding your classroom practices that will help you and your team members reflect on current assessment practices in your school.

Task Three: Review your findings and be prepared to discuss your survey with your team. Use these questions to guide your discussion:

1. Is one assessment type more prevalent than others?

2. What are the commonalities and differences among team members?

3. As a team, brainstorm ways to include assessments that are not currently evident or are used infrequently. How might you use the information from these assessments to inform your instruction?

Part 2—Standards, Curriculum, Instruction, and the Assessment Cycle

As mentioned in the Getting Started section, the movement toward standards-based assessment has led to a major paradigm shift in the way educators plan, instruct, and evaluate their students. We've established standards as the skills and knowledge students need to know at different points in their academic careers. The standards will vary according to grade level and content, as expectations change with student maturity. This graphic illustrates the cyclical relationship that exists among curriculum (content), instruction (process), and assessment (information) as aligned to the standards. This relationship creates an environment in which curriculum, instruction, and assessment reinforce one another.

Beginning with the standards, teachers establish the expected level of performance for their students and the appropriate sequence for the curriculum. From this, teachers can determine the best way to assess students to determine if proficiency is on target or achieved. Finally, teachers can project the best instructional methods to move students forward in their learning to achieve proficiency. This is a cyclic process based on the results of the assessments. Teachers may find there is a need to adjust instruction, which in turn leads to varying assessments. This is not a lock-step, one-time planning formula.

Curriculum and instruction need to be adjusted as frequently as necessary to make interventions and to ensure a forward momentum in student learning. In essence, it is almost impossible to say, "We mapped our curriculum," "I have completed my lesson plans," or "I have designed all of my assessments." It should be stated as "we are mapping our curriculum," "I am planning my instruction," and "I am designing my assessments." This is an ongoing and timely process based on student performance.

The alignment of standards in this cycle requires educators to have a thorough knowledge of the standards—their meaning and their implications. The expectations for learning required in the standards must be reflected in the curriculum, instruction, and assessment used in the classroom. Standards, grade level expectations, and their corresponding assessments are generally related to either Bloom's Taxonomy or Webb's Depth of Knowledge. The cognitive complexity associated with either Bloom or Webb maps out levels of performance expected for each of the standards and grade-level indicators or benchmarks. (See the *Side-by-Side View of Bloom's Taxonomy and Webb's Depth of Knowledge* and *Applying Bloom's Taxonomy* and *Applying Webb's Depth of Knowledge* in Appendix A.) It is imperative that teachers understand the language of their standards' frameworks, whether they are aligned to Bloom's, Webb's, or to another system for identifying depth and breadth of student learning and expectations for performance. *Applying Bloom's Taxonomy* and *Applying Webb's Depth of Knowledge* are two reference sets provided in Appendix A. These charts provide common verbs associated with each that are often reflected in standards documents and on large-scale assessment. For classroom application, each chart provides examples of activities and assessments that are aligned to the various levels of cognitive demand.

Bloom's Taxonomy is a classification of the cognitive objectives and skills that educators set for students. Educational objectives are divided into three domains: affective, psychomotor, and cognitive. The taxonomy is hierarchal, meaning that learning at the higher levels of cognition is dependent upon having attained prerequisite knowledge and skills at the lower levels. There is a new version of Bloom's that adds a seventh level and slightly adjusts the terminology. It reads: Remembering, understanding, applying, analyzing, evaluating, and creating.

Webb's Depth of Knowledge is an alignment method for examining the consistency between the cognitive demands of standards and the cognitive demands of assessments. Interpreting and assigning depth of knowledge levels to both objectives within standards and assessment items is an essential requirement of alignment analysis.

These models vary, but the common thread is the emphasis on the complexity of understanding and demonstration of knowledge expected of students. Instruction must hit these levels if performance by students is to be measured at the specific level indicated in the standards frameworks or grade level expectation. Educators need to know, understand, and use what is established as performance expectations in their state standards documents or frameworks and state assessments, district and school-level expectations, and all curriculum materials.

State standards and framework documents are not detailed enough at the middle school level to make direct instructional links without first determining exactly what students are to know and be able to do. Here's a sample standard for reading:

General Standard : Reading strategies for self-monitoring and adjusting reading
Student demonstrates ability to monitor comprehension for different types of text and purposes.

While this standard states what students need to be able to do, it is not written in language that is measurable at the classroom level or understandable to students. The standard must be broken down into specific skills and learning targets—achievement expectations for students.

Standard: Student demonstrates ability to monitor comprehension for different types of text and purposes.	Instructional Learning Targets	
	What students need to know	**What students are to be able to do**
Subset of full standard (benchmark) **Skills:** Use a range of self-monitoring and self-correction approaches (e.g. predicting and confirming, rereading, adjusting rate, sub-vocalizing, consulting, etc.) during independent reading.	• How to monitor for comprehension and self-check for understanding during independent reading.	• Use comprehension techniques, e.g., predicting. • Use foreshadowing and other devices to tell what will happen next in the text. • Use word clues to predict about the future. • Use character traits to determine the logical choice a character will make.

The key words for this standard are *monitor, comprehend, predict, adjust,* and *independent.* The key words indicate the expected student performance levels the targets need to address. Ask yourself, "At what level are students expected to demonstrate their understanding?" Some targets require simple comprehension by using words such as identify, list, and recall. Other targets, however, require deeper levels of student understanding with words such as apply, evaluate, justify, and analyze. Identifying these key words and the depth of understanding aligns the targets to the standard. Key words are pulled from Bloom's and Webb's cognitive complexities (see Appendix A). The key words in this standard indicate students are expected to use reading strategies independently to comprehend a variety of texts. The word "independent" indicates that the performance level for students is very deep. They are not being asked to define the term "predict," they are asked to use "predicting" as a strategy for reading comprehension during independent reading. This is application, not recall.

Once a standard has been broken down into subsets of skills and concepts, the instructional learning targets may be identified. These are measurable, but they are not in language students understand. The next step for the teacher is to create student-friendly learning targets in the form of "I can," "I am learning to," or "I am able to" statements.

Standard: Student demonstrates ability to monitor comprehension for different types of text and purposes	Instructional Learning Targets		Student Version of Target
	What students need to know	What students are to be able to do	Student-Friendly Language
Subset of full standard (benchmark) Skills: Use a range of self-monitoring and self-correction approaches (e.g., *predicting* and confirming, rereading, adjusting rate, sub-vocalizing, consulting, etc.) during independent reading	• How to monitor for comprehension and self-check for understanding during independent reading.	• Use comprehension techniques, e.g., predicting. • Use foreshadowing and other devices to tell what will happen next in the text. • Use word clues to *predict* about the future. • Use character traits to determine the logical choice a character will make.	Independently: • I can use words or other information from any text (book or story) to make a statement about what will happen next. • I can determine if my *prediction* is correct. • I can reread parts of the text if my *prediction* is not correct.

Through this process, teachers can determine the instructional progression necessary to move students forward in their achievement of a target. The instructional progression necessary for students to achieve a target may differ from classroom to classroom depending on the prior knowledge and experience of the students. Even within a given classroom, some students may need targets broken down further while other students, functioning at more advanced levels, may have some targets combined or accelerated. This is where differentiation plays an important role in understanding where students are in their learning relative to a standard.

With a deep understanding of the subsets of skills and concepts necessary to achieve a standard, teachers can choose the best assessment method to determine where students are in their learning in relation to a specific target. The information provided by assessment is then used to make timely instructional adjustments to ensure gaps in student learning do not materialize or broaden.

By taking these steps, alignment of assessment to targeted goals at the appropriate achievement level is more likely to occur. Also, providing students with a clear vision of the intended learning and what is expected of them increases student engagement.

Activity—Translating Standards into Meaningful Targets

Directions: Use the following tasks to focus on the importance of understanding standards and creating specific learning targets for instruction leading to the intended level of student understanding.

Task One: Review the Standards, Curriculum, Instruction, and Assessment Cycle below.

1. Discuss the interaction with standards for each: curriculum, instruction, and assessment.

2. How does the graphic explain the relationship of these key elements?

3. Why is this relationship critical?

4. How does this affect the individual learner?

Task Two: As a team, review the charts for Cognitive Complexity *(A Side-by-Side View of Bloom's Taxonomy & Webb's Depth of Knowledge)* and *Applying Webb's Depth of Knowledge* and *Applying Bloom's Taxonomy* provided in Appendix A. Discuss the similarities and differences between them. Investigate how your state's standards documents/frameworks are aligned. Why is knowing how your state framework is aligned to student performance expectations important for instructional and assessment purposes in your classroom?

Task Three: Work with a partner or as a cross grade-level content team to practice breaking down a standard and creating student-friendly learning targets. The step-by-step process is outlined below: *Turning Standards into Targets Guide.* Use the *Standard, Learning Target, and Assessment Template* that follows to record your work.

Turning Standards into Targets Guide

Group or team members are to use blank templates such as those on page 27, and follow the steps of creating targets as indicated below. These targets can then be posted in the classroom. At the middle school level, multiple targets are likely to be displayed as students learn to integrate skills.

We suggest you work as a team or with a partner the first time. One of the benefits of working in grade level or content teams is that every teacher will come away with the same expectations. Varied teaching techniques and strategies can be shared in the process. This makes for valuable team time on skills that cross content areas.

Steps:

1. Choose a standard and select a subset of the standard to record in the table on page 27.

2. Determine exactly what students are to know—put this in instructional language in the chart (noun).

3. Determine the Webb or Bloom level if it is not stated for you in your standards or framework document and enter this in the chart.

4. Determine and record critical vocabulary using the vocabulary that is built upon from previous instruction and the direct vocabulary pertinent to the new standard or skill being learned. Focus on the new vocabulary, but during instruction, reinforce other content vocabulary.

5. Rewrite the "verbs," or what students are to be able to do, into instructional language. Make sure it aligns with expected performance levels of Webb or Bloom. Now is a good time to review those performance levels to make sure your expectations are correct.

6. For the Student Target, rewrite the "to do" instructional language into student-friendly language. These become the learning targets that are shared with students prior to instruction. Grouping them as appropriate, post the targets in the room. It is important to remember that just posting the targets at the front of the room does not embed them into the instruction. Targets must be put into action and form the intentional guide for all instruction and assessment. Targets make the learning transparent for students.

Over time, some targets may become embedded expectations, e.g. targets associated with expectations for quality work or grammar, usage, and mechanics. In this instance, teachers may find it helpful to arrange these targets as reminders at work stations or centers around the classroom. Individual students who may struggle with or need more time to achieve particular targets benefit when they become personal targeted goals and are placed in their work folders or portfolios. These are then referred to periodically during conversations and conferences and through feedback.

When creating assessments, teachers should use the targets and the associated Bloom or Webb level as indicators about how best to assess relative to the targeted instruction. This process aligns to the standards and keeps instruction and learning focused and measurable. Results are then used for feedback (see Module III).

Subset of Standard or Grade Level Expectation:	Strand or Program of Study:		
	What students need to know (*noun*)	**What students are to be able to do** (*verb*)	**Student Target** (*use student-friendly language*)
DOK or Bloom's Level:			
Critical Vocabulary			

Module II
Assessment Methods and Item Design

Part 1—Assessment Methods

A balanced or comprehensive assessment system is one in which educators incorporate both high-quality summative assessment and formative assessment practices in their information-gathering and reporting process. Educators who are assessment literate select the most efficient and effective assessment to gather the information needed for a specific use and purpose. It is not the method or tool that determines whether the assessment is summative or formative; it is how the results are used. Educators need to deliberately choose assessment strategies that fit the learning targets and the level of cognitive complexity being assessed. They must also plan to gather information about student understanding formatively during the learning process to make instructional decisions in real time as well as design high quality summative assessments at the end of a learning cycle.

In Module I, we read about summative assessment, formative practice, standards, and learning targets. In Module II, we will investigate the different kinds of traditional assessment methods and their strengths and weaknesses. Traditionally, most assessments fall into one of four broad categories.

1. Selected response includes multiple-choice, true or false, and matching. Items in this category provide the correct answer, and students must "select" it from several options.
   - **Short answer falls between selected-response and writing assessments. Short-answer items require students to provide a response of several words, a list, or a few sentences.**

2. Writing assessments include constructed response, extended response, and essays. It is important to note that writing assessments in this category are considered as "writing on demand." These are not longer tasks that may take several drafts or that are researched and compiled over time, such as term papers. Writing over time is considered to be more of a performance task.

3. Performance assessments ask students to demonstrate skills and concepts through products. A "performance" could be working with a manipulative or responding to a probing question requesting an explanation of a problem-solving technique. A performance could be a longer term project in which students are asked to incorporate multiple standards and create presentations, research papers, or demonstrations based on their learning. These are sometimes used in group projects.

4. Personal communication includes questions and answers, conferences, interviews, and oral examinations, all of which are an integral part of the information-gathering process.

Assessment Items: Use and Expectations

	Selected Response	Constructed Response	Performance Events, Tasks, Portfolios
Student Task	Select answers	Create or write answers	Create complex product
Time Necessary to Respond	Within one class period	Within one class period	One or more class periods
Scoring	Right or wrong based on key	Requires a scoring guide	Requires a scoring guide, possibly more than one, dependent on criteria
Characteristic	Most often used to assess knowledge or recall. Higher order multiple choice items are generally not used at the classroom level.	Some depth, Can be open to a range of or multiple correct responses.	Greater depth; requires thought and work over time; can be used to monitor progress and student growth
Insights into Student Understanding	Reveals what students do not know	Reveals what students know and can do	Reveals what students know and can do

Adapted and used with permission from the *CCSSO~SCASS Health Education Assessment Project*

The chart illustrates characteristics of three of the assessment methods mentioned previously. Each method falls into categories of use and expectations. It is important to choose the best assessment method to determine the level of student performance and understanding as outlined in the state standards' frameworks and addressed in specific learning targets. The characteristic of each assessment category gives insight into the depth of understanding (see Webb's Depth of Knowledge and Bloom's Taxonomy in Appendix A) that can be expected from the student if this type of assessment is used.

For example, a multiple-choice item may be written to assess higher order thinking, but it is most often used at the classroom level to assess or determine knowledge level or recall of information. When a multiple-choice item is used as a method to determine what students do not know—is the response right or wrong and whether or not students know the information, it is an effective and efficient way for teachers to make a quick analysis before moving on with their instruction.

Constructed-response questions require students to explain or demonstrate their thinking or reasoning. There generally is a range of acceptable responses that are reflected in a rubric or scoring guide. It is important to anticipate how students may respond to a constructed-response item and build this information into scoring notes. Performance assessments or portfolios, which take more than one class period to complete, have greater depth and truly reveal what students know and can do. These methods assess higher levels of cognitive demand and are effective ways to monitor progress and student growth over time.

In addition to choosing the most effective assessment method, there are also design considerations. These will be discussed in Part 2.

Activity: Assessment Methods, Strengths, and Weaknesses

Directions: Use the following tasks to focus on the importance of utilizing a variety of assessment methods to provide students with the opportunity to reach their learning targets.

Task One: Meet with your team and complete the *Analysis of Various Assessment Methods* chart below. The first assessment method is completed as a model to get you started.

Analysis of Various Assessment Methods

Use the information provided in Module II to assist with this activity.

Assessment Method	Advantages	Disadvantages	Comments
Selected Response	• less time to administer • less time to grade • good for assessing knowledge targets	• allows guessing • doesn't show student work • not a good method for "higher-order" cognitive targets	• provides correct answer • difficult to create meaningful distractors
Writing			
Short Answer			
Performance			
Personal Communication			

Task Two: In Module I, Part I, you completed a survey in which you listed the different types of assessment (pre-instructional, formative, and summative) you use in the classroom.

Specific Assessment Methods Used in the Classroom

Based on your responses to the survey, indicate the specific assessment methods used in your classroom.

Pre-Instructional	Assessment Method
	Selected Response
	Writing
	Short Answer
	Performance
	Personal Communication

Formative	Assessment Method
	Selected Response
	Writing
	Short Answer
	Performance
	Personal Communication

Summative	Assessment Method
	Selected Response
	Writing
	Short Answer
	Performance
	Personal Communication

What do your responses tell you about your assessment practices? Do you depend on one type of assessment method more than others? Should changes be made? Why or why not?

Part 2—Item Purpose and Design

Any assessment used in the classroom, whether it is teacher-generated or from other sources (e.g., textbooks, pre-made assessments, programs), must be aligned to the standards or targets that are the focus of the instruction. The assessments must be aligned to the expected level of performance as outlined in the state content frameworks and grade level indicators or benchmarks, and they should incorporate the same language that is used during instruction.

Different assessment methods serve different purposes for information gathering. We know that if we want to assess students' ability to *recall* detailed information, a selected response item is often the most effective and efficient way to do so. If we want to determine whether students can *explain* a process or *justify* their reasoning, we must provide a different type of assessment. One way would be through oral communication, simply asking the students to explain to you how they came up with an answer. Another is to ask students to respond in writing.

One of the writing assessment methods is constructed response. Because this method of assessment generally provides solid information about student understanding and can be completed within one class period, we will concentrate on it in this section. The following is a list of basic design considerations for constructed-response questions:

- If the item asks students to read a passage or examine a graphic and then "give three ways" or "explain two reasons" based on the material given, make sure there are at least three ways or two reasons found in the material provided.

- If you want the students to provide examples, the directions to the students should tell them specifically to provide examples and how many to provide.

- If you want the students to identify information, do not ask them to discuss, describe, or explain.

- Even if the item has a graphic, there still must be a prompt that describes or provides information related to the graphic or item directions.

- Present the prompt in paragraph or prose form.

- Use bullets or highlighted or bold print to emphasize the details in the prompt.

- If the students are required to respond to multiple parts of a question, label each part separately (a, b, c).

- Every item needs to be error and bias free. Make sure there is no language that may confuse students or create a bias based on culture, ethnicity, or native language.

Sample Constructed-Response Item for Middle Level Science:

DOK: 2 or Bloom: Application

A light ray travels through air in a straight line until it hits the surface of a piece of clear glass, as shown in the diagram below.

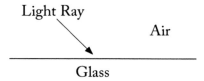

a. Draw two diagrams. In each diagram, show one thing that could happen to the ray of light after it hits the glass surface.
b. For each of your diagrams, describe one example of a way people make use of the fact that light behaves the way your diagram shows.

This sample item follows all of the basic design elements provided in the bulleted list. In addition to the elements listed for consideration, please note how easy this item is to read and how clear and simple the diagram is. There should be no mystery about what the task requests. Students should not have to spend time trying to figure out what they are supposed to do. This interferes with the quality of their responses. You will be asked to analyze this item in a task following this module.

One of the considerations in designing a constructed-response item is the use of action words (e.g., describe, illustrate, compare). These words must be used in alignment with the intended standards or targets because they require a specific form of action based on a level of cognitive complexity (refer to your standards documents to interpret the action words and their cognitive complexity, and please refer to the *Applying Bloom's Taxonomy* and *Applying Webb's Depth of Knowledge* charts in Appendix A). Any assessment item must align to the intended target and measure student understanding at the expected performance level. In very simple terms, the quality and level of the response students provide is dictated by how and what they are asked to do.

Students need to know what these action words mean, and students need to know what is expected of them when they read specific action words. Students also need to be provided with exemplars of the range of possible and acceptable responses. Prior to students answering any constructed-response items, they need to learn how to read them with special attention to action words and how to respond to them. A sequence of modeling, practice, and review is the best way to accomplish this. Providing exemplars of the different levels represented in a scoring guide or rubric also helps students visualize what acceptable responses look like for each of the score points. Eventually, this process assists students in improving their ability to self-assess and self-monitor.

One of the attributes important to a constructed-response assessment is openness. Openness refers to how much information is requested. If an item is too open, it will take students too long to respond. If this is the level of understanding and response you expect, then a different type of assessment is recommended. For example, you may want to consider a performance task. If the item is too closed, the student responses will be too short. Again, you may want to consider a different form of assessment, such as short answer. Please refer to the *Side-by-Side Chart View of Bloom's Taxonomy* and *Webb's Depth of Knowledge* in Appendix A for insight into an appropriate length of time to plan for student responses depending on the cognitive demand of the intended target. Constructed-response items often leave opportunity for students to demonstrate their understanding in a variety of ways. Importance is placed on the quality of the support students provide for their responses.

Scoring Rubrics or Guides

A constructed-response item is not complete unless there is a scoring rubric or guide that corresponds to the expected level of performance and takes into consideration the varying ways a student may respond. It is necessary to anticipate the varying responses and how students will be scored if they respond to only a portion of the question correctly. Scoring rubrics provide the teacher with written guidelines for scoring student responses to a specific prompt or question.

General rubrics or guides provide the student with expectations for performance at each score point. As mentioned previously, it is best to have exemplars for each score point to assist students in understanding where they are relative to the highest score. This also assists them in their self-assessment process. Teachers can gather samples of student work for the different levels of a general scoring rubric or guide to save as exemplars. Important considerations for a scoring rubric include alignment and the number of score points needed as described below.

Alignment: The scoring rubric must be aligned with the intent of the learning target and the item (question). This means that the language for items such as verb choices and numbers should be consistent.

Number of Score Points: Determine the number of score points based on the depth of the prompt or question. Each score point must provide a description of performance. It is not necessary to reinvent a scoring rubric for each task, but it is important for students to understand what is expected of them through modeling and exemplars related to each level. It is fine to have a task with a three point rubric (0, #1, #2), some with a four-point rubric (0,#1,#2,#3), and others with a five-point rubric (0,#1,#2,#3,#4) as long as students understand ahead of time which rubric will be used.

Sample General Scoring Rubric or Guide for Constructed Response

This general scoring rubric includes major characteristics for each of the score points.

Score	Description
4	Student completes all important components of the item and communicates ideas clearly. Response demonstrates in-depth understanding of the relevant concepts and/or process. Where appropriate, student chooses more efficient and/or sophisticated processes. Where appropriate, student offers insightful interpretations or extensions (generalizations, applications, analogies). **Key words used in the description: in-depth, thorough, detailed, complete, sophisticated**
3	Student completes most components of the item and communicates clearly. Response demonstrates an understanding of major concepts even though student overlooks or misunderstands some less-important ideas or details. **Key words used in the description: general, broad, fairly sound**
2	Student completes some important components of the item and communicates those clearly. Response demonstrates that there are gaps in the student's conceptual understanding. **Key words used in the description: limited, partial, simplistic, basic, rudimentary**
1	Student addresses only a small portion of the question. **Key words used in the description: little, minimal, inadequate**
0	Response is incorrect or contains some correct work that is irrelevant to the skill or concept being measured. **Note: This description is not used in all rubrics.**
Blank	No response. **Note: This description is not used in all rubrics.**

An item-specific rubric will use the same characteristics as a general rubric but is based on the specific item and provides notes and specific information to assist in using the rubric or guide when reviewing student responses.

Scoring Rubric or Guide Adjusted Specifically for the Sample Science Item

Score	Description
4	The student correctly (a) draws diagrams showing two things the light ray could do after reaching the glass surface, and (b) describes a use of each light behavior shown in the diagrams. There are no errors.
3	The student (a) draws diagrams showing reflection and transmission but is not precise in the angles of reflection and refraction, and (b) describes uses of the two light behaviors with some lack of detail or clarity.
2	The student (a) draws one diagram that correctly shows a way the light ray responds to the surface, and (b) describes a way that behavior is used. **or** The student draws two diagrams that are partly correct and attempts to describe a use for each but makes major errors. **or** The student only draws two diagrams that are mostly correct.
1	The student attempts Part a or Part b but is mostly wrong. Shows only minimal understanding.
0	Response is incorrect or contains some correct work that is irrelevant to the skill or concept being measured.
Blank	No response.

It is also a good idea to generate scoring notes for yourself or for students to use when they self or peer assess. This becomes a guide to the range of acceptable answers. An example based on the Sample Science Item follows.

Scoring Notes and Information

Part a: Three things can happen to the ray of light.

- It can reflect from the surface with the angle of incidence being equal to the angle of reflection.

- It can refract as it is transmitted through the surface with the ray bending toward the perpendicular (normal) to the surface.

- It can be absorbed at the surface (it is improbable this alternative would be recognized at this level) and become heat within the glass.

Part b: Reflection is used to create images in flat mirrors, to focus light with curved mirrors, and for many other uses. Refraction is used to correct sight with glasses, to magnify images, to separate colors (prisms), and for many other uses.

Constructed-response items are often used as part of a traditional paper-and-pencil summative assessment. Their usefulness in the formative assessment process is often overlooked. Here are some suggestions on how to use constructed-response items formatively.

- As an **Exit Slip** at the end of a class period. Teachers can review student responses and make the appropriate instructional adjustments the next day. This also provides an opportunity for feedback. This can be accomplished in a whole class format by using several examples from the student responses to explain a point about the work, addressing specific comments to individual students during mini-conferences, or pulling students together for small group instruction.

- As **Homework** practice or extension of learning. The next day, put students in pairs to go over the constructed-response item using the corresponding scoring rubric. Students can use each other as instructional resources and provide feedback to each other about their work.

Activity: Analysis of a Constructed-Response Item

Task One: Based on the grade level or the content area(s) of your team, work individually or in pairs. Review the sample constructed-response science item provided previously, and complete the Analysis of a Constructed-Response Item below.

Analysis of a Constructed-Response Item

Use the chart below to deconstruct the various design elements of the sample science item provided in Module II Part 2.

Design Element	Example from Sample Science Item
If the item asks students to read a passage or examine a graphic and then "give three ways" or "explain two reasons" based on the material given, make sure there are three ways or two reasons found in the material provided.	
If you want the students to provide examples, the directions to the students should tell them to provide examples and how many.	
If you want the students to identify information, do not ask them to discuss, describe or explain.	
Even if the item has a graphic, there still must be a prompt that describes or provides information related to the graphic and/or item directions.	
Present the prompt in paragraph or prose form.	
Use bullets, highlights, or bold print to emphasize the details in the prompt.	
If the students are required to respond to multiple parts of a question, label each part separately (a, b, c).	

Task Two: Individually, follow the same analysis process on a constructed-response item of your own design or one provided in a resource you frequently use. Use the chart below as a guide.

Analysis of a Constructed-Response Item

Design Element	Example from Item
If the item asks students to read a passage or examine a graphic and then "give three ways" or "explain two reasons" based on the material given, make sure there are three ways or two reasons found in the material provided.	
If you want the students to provide examples, the directions to the students should tell them to provide examples and how many.	
If you want the students to identify information, do not ask them to discuss, describe or explain.	
Even if the item has a graphic, there still must be a prompt that describes or provides information related to the graphic and/or item directions.	
Present the prompt in paragraph or prose form.	
Use bullets, highlights, or bold print to emphasize the details in the prompt.	
If the students are required to respond to multiple parts of a question, label each part separately (a, b, c).	

Task Three: Meet with your team and share the results of Task Two.

1. Based on this work, what are some of the changes you would consider in the purpose and design of your existing items?

2. What steps can you take to ensure this is done for all constructed-response items used in your classroom?

Module III
Formative Assessment in the Classroom

Part 1—Defining Formative Assessment

A committee affiliated with the Council of Chief State School Officers (CCSSO) Formative Assessment for Students and Teachers (FAST) created the following definition, which has become widely accepted:

> "Formative assessment is a process used by teachers and students during instruction that provides feedback to adjust ongoing teaching and learning to improve students' achievement of intended outcomes."

There are key points in this definition of formative assessment that we need to consider. First, formative assessment is a process not a product. Formative assessment is not something that can be purchased and "given" to students to "test" them. There are many tools (e.g., graphic organizers, activities, and ancillary materials associated with programs or texts) that can be used formatively, but they are not formative until the information gathered from them is used to provide feedback to students about their learning and to adjust instruction. Second, formative assessment is instructional practice that involves both teachers and students and that requires students to be active "partners" throughout the instruction and learning process.

If the classroom practice of formative assessment is to be effective, it needs to be a means for students to understand their learning, identify misconceptions, and formulate clear ways to improve and move their learning forward. Typically, the results of classroom assessment are not used for this purpose. Students are more often viewed as the "objects" of tests. Tests happen to students after the instruction has occurred. In this sense, testing is a snapshot of student learning rather than a video stream of learning as it occurs (Heritage, 2007).

Another key point in the definition of formative assessment is that it is pedagogy, an integral part of the instructional process. The information gathered from formative assessment is used as feedback for teachers and students. This feedback, whether generated by the teacher or by students, provides insight into student understanding and into where students are in their learning relative to intended outcomes.

In formative assessment classroom practice, students learn how to self-assess by using established criteria and exemplars and to work with their peers to assess learning based on established learning intentions. Students then reflect on their learning and monitor their learning progress. As a result, students become engaged through self-regulation and through setting the goals for their own learning (Sadler, 1989). For many teachers and students, this kind of student involvement requires a major shift in how they view assessment and instruction. It also requires a major shift in the relationship between students and teachers. Students are no longer viewed as receptacles for information and tested for their learning of this information. They are seen as active partners in the instruction, learning, and assessment process. Assessment, then, becomes an intentional, instructional process, and the information gathered from it is used purposefully to move student learning forward and to engage students as actors in and owners of this learning.

Although many of the instructional practices generally associated with formative assessment (e.g., observation, questioning, having students work together, establishing learning goals) are not new to teachers, the level and kind of implementation is what separates effective practice from "just doing it." In fact, it is easy to say, "I already do that" and stop there without truly reflecting on current practice. However, when we respond in this way, nothing changes. Instructional practice and the level of student learning remain the same. What we need to ask is, "How do we collect information about student learning? How do we share this information with students? How are students involved in gathering and using information about their own learning? How do we, as teachers, use this information to adjust our instruction to more closely address the specific learning needs of our students?" There are unfortunate consequences to not asking and not trying to answer these questions.

Research indicates that the practice of formative assessment is not widespread. One clear reason is that many teachers do not understand that formative assessment is pedagogy as opposed to a specific testing event. There is, however, ample evidence indicating that formative assessment, done with intent and clear purpose, has a dramatic, positive impact on student learning. Research also indicates that students become engaged in their learning and take responsibility for this learning when formative assessment practices are adopted and become part of classroom culture. (Black & Wiliam, 2003)

The **Five Key Strategies** of effective formative assessment practices are listed in the article *Classroom Assessment: Minute by Minute, Day by Day*. This article is assigned in an activity at the end of this module. The five key formative assessment strategies are

1. Clarifying learning intentions and sharing criteria for success.

2. Engineering effective classroom discussions, questions, and learning tasks that elicit evidence of learning.

3. Providing feedback that moves learners forward.

4. Activating students as the owners of their own learning.

5. Activating students as instructional resources for each other.

While each of these strategies is important, it is their interrelationship that makes formative assessment such a powerful process for improving student learning. To provide direction and guidance to the teacher and to students, the practice of formative assessment must initially focus on clarifying learning intentions and sharing criteria for success. This sharing is the foundation for all of the formative classroom assessment strategies. Student-friendly learning targets were discussed in Module 1.

Based on the learning intentions, or learning targets, and the established criteria for success associated with them, teachers are then better able to plan for and implement the lessons, activities, tasks, observations, questions, and discussions that will move students forward and assist them in achieving the intended learning. Learning targets should form the basis for all classroom assessment, and each classroom activity needs to be directed toward the targeted learning goal that is shared with students prior to instruction.

Carefully orchestrated series of instructional practices leading to clear learning targets provide opportunities for feedback for the teacher and for the student. When teachers provide students with descriptive feedback based on the students' progress toward reaching these established learning targets, students are far better able to gain insight into errors, misconceptions, and clues about how to improve their learning. Effective feedback can be provided by the teacher or by a peer. Furthermore, involving peers as instructional resources helps students in a reciprocal fashion to reach deeper levels of understanding (Heritage, 2007). When all of these formative assessment strategies are combined creatively and with intention in the classroom, students become more actively engaged in their own learning and in the learning of their peers as opposed to being passive containers waiting to be filled.

Activity 1: Professional Inquiry

Directions: In the past few years, research and associated writings about formative assessment have come to the forefront in most educational publications. As part of your professional inquiry into formative assessment as practice, we have provided on pages 46–55 one article as a starting point as required reading. Conduct a Web search using *Formative Assessment* as the key phrase. Choose a minimum of two other articles to read and share with your team. As you conduct your research, begin to formulate how these practices could become part of your everyday routine and classroom culture.

Task One: After reading two or more articles, complete the *Article Report* on the next page. Create a list of the most significant findings from the articles. Use the questions to guide your thinking.

Task Two: Meet with your team and share your findings. Add the team responses from the articles you did not read. Discuss how your findings can influence your practice.

Article Report

Work individually to complete Task One. Work as a team to complete Task Two

Name of the Article	Most Significant Findings	Why Is This Important?
Article 1—*Classroom Assessment: Minute by Minute, Day by Day* **Questions:** What aspects of your current practice are reflected in this article? What makes these *formative assessment* strategies and techniques instead of just good teaching techniques?		
Additional Articles:		

Classroom Assessment: Minute by Minute, Day by Day
Siobhan Leahy, Christine Lyon, Marnie Thompson and Dylan Wiliam

In classrooms that use assessment to support learning, teachers continually adapt instruction to meet student needs.

There is intuitive appeal in using assessment to support instruction: assessment for learning rather than assessment *of* learning. We have to test our students for many reasons. Obviously, such testing should be useful in guiding teaching. Many schools formally test students at the end of a marking period—that is, every 6 to 10 weeks—but the information from such tests is hard to use, for two reasons.

First, only a small amount of testing time can be allotted to each standard or skill covered in the marking period. Consequently, the test is better for monitoring overall levels of achievement than for diagnosing specific weaknesses.

Second, the information arrives too late to be useful. We can use the results to make broad adjustments to curriculum, such as reteaching or spending more time on a unit, or identifying teachers who appear to be especially successful at teaching particular units. But if educators are serious about using assessment to improve instruction, then we need more fine-grained assessments, and we need to use the information they yield to modify instruction as we teach.

Changing Gears
What we need is a shift from *quality control* in learning to quality assurance. Traditional approaches to instruction and assessment involve teaching some given material, and then, at the end of teaching, working out who has and hasn't learned it—akin to a quality control approach in manufacturing. In contrast, assessment *for* learning involves adjusting teaching as needed while the learning is still taking place—a quality assurance approach. Quality assurance also involves a shift of attention from teaching to learning. The emphasis is on what the students are getting out of the process rather than on what teachers are putting into it, reminiscent of the old joke that schools are places where children go to watch teachers work.

In a classroom that uses assessment to support learning, the divide between instruction and assessment blurs. Everything students do—such as conversing in groups, completing seatwork, answering and asking questions, working on projects, handing in homework assignments, even sitting silently and looking confused—is a potential source of information about how much they understand. The teacher who consciously uses assessment to support learning takes in this information, analyzes it, and makes instructional decisions that address the understandings and misunderstandings that these assessments reveal. The amount of information can be overwhelming—one teacher likened it to "negotiating a swiftly flowing river"—so a key part of using assessment for learning is figuring out how to hone in on a manageable range of alternatives.

Research indicates that using assessment for learning improves student achievement. About seven years ago, Paul Black and one of us, Dylan Wiliam, found that students taught by teachers who used assessment for learning achieved in six or seven months what would otherwise have taken a year (1998). More important, these improvements appeared to be consistent across countries (including Canada, England, Israel, Portugal, and the United States), as well as across age brackets and content areas. We also found, after working with teachers in England, that these gains in achievement could be sustained over extended periods of time. The gains even held up when we measured student achievement with externally mandated standardized tests (see Wiliam, Lee, Harrison, & Black, 2004).

Using this research and these ideas as a starting point, we and other colleagues at Educational Testing Service (ETS) have been working for the last two years with elementary, middle, and high school teachers in Arizona, Delaware, Maryland, Massachusetts, New Jersey, New Mexico, and Pennsylvania. We have deepened our understanding of how assessment for learning can work in U.S. classrooms, and we have learned from teachers about the challenges of integrating assessment into classroom instruction.

Our Work with Teachers

In 2003 and 2004, we explored a number of ways of introducing teachers to the key ideas of assessment for learning. In one model, we held a three-day workshop during the summer in which we introduced teachers to the main ideas of assessment for learning and the research that shows that it works. We then shared specific techniques that teachers could use in their classrooms to bring assessment to life. During the subsequent school year, we met monthly with these teachers, both to learn from them what really worked in their classrooms and to offer suggestions about ways in which they might develop their practice. We also observed their classroom practices to gauge the extent to which they were implementing assessment-forlearning techniques and to determine the effects that these techniques were having on student learning. In other models, we spaced out the three days of the summer institute over several months (for example, one day in March, one in April, and one in May) so that teachers could try out some of the techniques in their classes between meetings.

As we expected, different teachers found different techniques useful; what worked for some did not work for others. This confirmed for us that there could be no one-size-fits-all package. However, we did find a set of five broad strategies to be equally powerful for teachers of all content areas and at all grade levels:

- Clarifying and sharing learning intentions and criteria for success.

- Engineering effective classroom discussions, questions, and learning tasks.

- Providing feedback that moves learners forward.

- Activating students as the owners of their own learning.

- Activating students as instructional resources for one another.

We think of these strategies as nonnegotiable in that they define the territory of assessment for learning. More important, we know from the research and from our work with teachers that these strategies are desirable things to do in any classroom.

However, the way in which a teacher might implement one of these strategies with a particular class or at a particular time requires careful thought. A self-assessment technique that works for students learning math in the middle grades may not work in a 2nd grade writing lesson. Moreover, what works for one 7th grade pre-algebra class may not work for the 7th grade prealgebra class down the hall because of differences in the students or teachers.

Given this variability, it is important to offer teachers a range of techniques for each strategy, making them responsible for deciding which techniques they will use and allowing them time and freedom to customize these techniques to meet the needs of their students.

Teachers have tried out, adapted, and invented dozens of techniques, reporting on the results in meetings and interviews (to date, we have cataloged more than 50 techniques, and we expect the list to expand to more than 100 in the coming year). Many of these techniques require only subtle changes in practice, yet research on the underlying strategies suggests that they have a high "gearing"—meaning that these small changes in practice can leverage large gains in student learning (see Black & Wiliam, 1998; Wiliam, 2005). Further, the teaching practices that support these strategies are low-tech, low-cost, and usually feasible for individual teachers to implement.In this way, they differ dramatically from large-scale interventions, such as class size reduction or curriculum overhauls. We offer here a brief sampling of techniques for implementing each of the five assessment-for-learning strategies.

Clarify and Share Intentions and Criteria

Low achievement is often the result of students failing to understand what teachers require of them (Black & Wiliam, 1998). Many teachers address this issue by posting the state standard or learning objective in a prominent place at the start of the lesson, but such an approach is rarely successful because the standards are not written in student-friendly language.

Teachers in our various projects have explored many ways of making their learning objectives and their criteria for success transparent to students. One common method involves circulating work samples, such as lab reports, that a previous year's class completed, in view of prompting a discussion about quality. Students decide which reports are good and analyze what's good about the good ones and what's lacking in the weaker ones. Teachers have also found that by choosing the samples carefully, they can tune the task to the capabilities of the class. Initially, a teacher might choose four or five samples at very different quality levels to get students to focus on broad criteria for quality. As students grow more skilled, however, teachers can challenge them with a number of samples of similar quality to force the students to become more critical and reflective.

Engineer Effective Classroom Discussion

Many teachers spend a considerable proportion of their instructional time in whole-class discussion or question-and-answer sessions, but these sessions tend to rehearse existing knowledge rather than create new knowledge for students. Moreover, teachers generally listen for the "correct" answer instead of listening for what they can learn about the students' thinking; as Davis (1997) says, they listen *evaluatively* rather than interpretively. The teachers with whom we have worked have tried to address this issue by asking students questions that either prompt students to think or provide teachers with information that they can use to adjust instruction to meet learning needs.

As a result of this focus, teachers have become aware of the need to carefully plan the questions that they use in class. Many of our teachers now spend more time planning instruction than grading student work, a practice that emphasizes the shift from quality control to quality assurance. By thinking more carefully about the questions they ask in class, teachers can check on students' understanding while the students are still in the class rather than after they have left, as is the case with grading.

Some questions are designed as "range-finding" questions to reveal what students know at the beginning of an instructional sequence. For example, a high school biology teacher might ask the class how much water taken up by the roots of a corn plant is lost through transpiration. Many students believe that transpiration is "bad" and that plants try to minimize the amount of water lost in this process, whereas, in fact, the "lost" water plays an important role in transporting nutrients around the plant.

A middle school mathematics teacher might ask students to indicate how many fractions they can find between 1/6 and 1/7. Some students will think there aren't any; others may suggest an answer that, although in some way understandable, is an incorrect use of mathematical notation, such as 1 over 6½. The important feature of such range-finding items is that they can help a teacher judge where to begin instruction.

Of course, teachers can use the same item in a number of ways, depending on the context. They could use the question about fractions at the end of a sequence of instruction on equivalent fractions to see whether students have grasped the main idea. A middle school science teacher might ask students at the end of a laboratory experiment, "What was the dependent variable in today's lab?" A social studies teacher, at the end of a project on World War II, might ask students to state their views about which year the war began and give reasons supporting their choice.

Teachers can also use questions to check on student understanding before continuing the lesson. We call this a "hinge point" in the lesson because the lesson can go in different directions, depending on student responses. By explicitly integrating these hinge points into instruction, teachers can make their teaching more responsive to their students' needs in real time.

However, no matter how good the hinge-point question, the traditional model of classroom questioning presents two additional problems. The first is lack of engagement. If the classroom rule dictates that students raise their hands to answer questions, then students can disengage from the classroom by keeping their hands down. For this reason, many of our teachers have instituted the idea of "no hands up, except to ask a question." The teacher can either decide whom to call on to answer a question or use some randomizing device, such as a beaker of Popsicle sticks with the students' names written on them. This way, all students know that they need to stay engaged because the teacher could call on any one of them. One teacher we worked with reported that her students love the fairness of this approach and that her shyer students are showing greater confidence as a result of being invited to participate in this way. Other teachers have said that some students think it's unfair that they don't get a chance to show off when they know the answer.

The second problem with traditional questioning is that the teacher gets to hear only one student's thinking. To gauge the understanding of the whole class, the teacher needs to get responses from all the students in real time. One way to do this is to have all students write their answers on individual dry-erase boards, which they hold up at the teacher's request. The teacher can then scan responses for novel solutions as well as misconceptions. This technique would be particularly helpful with the fraction question we cited.

Another approach is to give each student a set of four cards labeled *A, B, C,* and *D,* and ask the question in multiple-choice format. If the question is well designed, the teacher can quickly judge the different levels of understanding in the class. If all students answer correctly, the teacher can move on. If no one answers correctly, the teacher might choose to reteach the concept. If some students answer correctly and some answer incorrectly, the teacher can use that knowledge to engineer a whole-class discussion on the concept or match up the students for peer teaching. Hinge-point questions provide a window into students' thinking and, at the same time, give the teacher some ideas about how to take the students' learning forward.

Provide Feedback That Moves Learners Forward

After the lesson, of course, comes grading. The problem with giving a student a grade and a supportive comment is that these practices don't cause further learning. Before they began thinking about assessment for learning, none of the teachers with whom we worked believed that their students spent as long considering teacher feedback as it had taken the teachers to provide that feedback. Indeed, the research shows that when students receive a grade and a comment, they ignore the comment (see Butler, 1988). The first thing they look at is the grade, and the second thing they look at is their neighbor's grade.

To be effective, feedback needs to cause thinking. Grades don't do that. Scores don't do that. And comments like "Good job" don't do that either. What *does* cause thinking is a comment that addresses what the student needs to do to improve, linked to rubrics where appropriate. Of course, it's difficult to give insightful comments when the assignment asked for 20 calculations or 20 historical dates, but even in these cases, feedback can cause thinking. For example, one approach that many of our teachers have found productive is to say to a student, "Five of these 20 answers are incorrect. Find them and fix them!"

Some of our teachers worried about the extra time needed to provide useful feedback. But once students engaged in self-assessment and peer assessment, the teachers were able to be more selective about which elements of student work they looked at, and they could focus on giving feedback that peers were unable to provide.

Teachers also worried about the reactions of administrators and parents. Some teachers needed waivers from principals to vary school policy (for example, to give comments rather than grades on interim assessments). Most principals were happy to permit these changes once teachers explained their reasons. Parents were also supportive. Some even said they found comments more useful than grades because the comments provided them with guidance on how to help their children.

Activate Students as Owners of Their Learning

Developing assessment for learning in one's classroom involves altering the implicit contract between teacher and students by creating shared responsibility for learning. One simple technique is to distribute green and red "traffic light" cards, which students "flash" to indicate their level of understanding (green = understand, red = don't understand). A teacher who uses this technique with her 9th grade algebra classes told us that one day she moved on too quickly, without scanning the students' cards. A student picked up her own card as well as her neighbors' cards, waved them in the air, and pointed at them wildly, with the red side facing the teacher. The teacher considered this ample proof that this student was taking ownership of her learning.

Students also take ownership of their learning when they assess their own work, using agreed-on criteria for success. Teachers can provide students with a rubric written in student-friendly language, or the class can develop the rubric with the teacher's guidance (for examples, see Black, Harrison, Lee, Marshall, &

Wiliam, 2003). The teachers we have worked with report that students' self-assessments are generally accurate, and students say that assessing their own work helped them understand the material in a new way.

Activate Students as Instructional Resources for One Another

Getting students started with self-assessment can be challenging. Many teachers provide students with rubrics but find that the students seem unable to use the rubrics to focus and improve their work. For many students, using a rubric to assess their own work is just too difficult. But as most teachers know, students from kindergarten to 12th grade are much better at spotting errors in other students' work than in their own work. For that reason, peer assessment and feedback can be an important part of effective instruction. Students who get feedback are not the only beneficiaries. Students who give feedback also benefit, sometimes more than the recipients. As they assess the work of a peer, they are forced to engage in understanding the rubric, but in the context of someone else's work, which is less emotionally charged. Also, students often communicate more effectively with one another than the teacher does, and the recipients of the feedback tend to be more engaged when the feedback comes from a peer. When the teacher gives feedback, students often just "sit there and take it" until the ordeal is over.

Using peer and self-assessment techniques frees up teacher time to plan better instruction or work more intensively with small groups of students. It's also a highly effective teaching strategy. One cautionary note is in order, however. In our view, students should not be giving another student a grade that will be reported to parents or administrators. Peer assessment should be focused on improvement, not on grading.

Using Evidence of Learning to Adapt Instruction

One final strategy binds the others together: Assessment information should be used to adapt instruction to meet student needs.

As teachers listen to student responses to a hinge-point question or note the prevalence of red or green cards, they can make on-the-fly decisions to review material or to pair up those who understand the concept with those who don't for some peer tutoring. Using the evidence they have elicited, teachers can make instructional decisions that they otherwise could not have made.

At the end of the lesson, many of the teachers with whom we work use "exit passes." Students are given index cards and must turn in their responses to a question posed by the teacher before they can leave the classroom. Sometimes this will be a "big idea" question, to check on the students' grasp of the content of the lesson. At other times, it will be a range-finding question, to help the teacher judge where to begin the next day's instruction.

Teachers using assessment for learning continually look for ways in which they can generate evidence of student learning, and they use this evidence to adapt their instruction to better meet their students' learning needs. They share the responsibility for learning with the learners; students know that they are responsible for alerting the teacher when they do not understand. Teachers design their instruction to yield evidence about student achievement; for example, they carefully craft hinge-point questions to create "moments of contingency," in which the direction of the instruction will depend on student responses. Teachers provide feedback that engages students, make time in class for students to work on improvement, and activate students as instructional resources for one another.

All this sounds like a lot of work, but according to our teachers, it doesn't take any more time than the practices they used to engage in. And these techniques are far more effective. Teachers tell us that they are enjoying their teaching more.

Supporting Teacher Change
None of these ideas is new, and a large and growing research base shows that implementing them yields substantial improvement in student learning. So why are these strategies and techniques not practiced more widely? The answer is that knowing about these techniques and strategies is one thing; figuring out how to make them work in your own classroom is something else.

That's why we're currently developing a set of tools and workshops to support teachers in developing a deep and practical understanding of assessment for learning, primarily through the vehicle of school-based teacher learning communities. After we introduce teachers to the basic principles of assessment for learning, we encourage them to try out two or three techniques in their own classrooms and to meet with other colleagues regularly—ideally every month—to discuss their experiences and see what the other teachers are doing (see Black, Harrison, Lee, Marshall, & Wiliam, 2003, 2004). Teachers are accountable because they know they will have to share their experiences with their colleagues. However, each teacher is also in control of what he or she tries out. Over time, the teacher learning community develops a shared language that enables teachers to talk to one another about what they are doing. Teachers build individual and collective skill and confidence in assessment for learning. Colleagues help them decide when it is time to move on to the next challenge as well as point out potential pitfalls.

In many ways, the teacher learning community approach is similar to the larger assessment-forlearning approach. Both focus on where learners are now, where they want to go, and how we can help them get there.

References

Black, P., Harrison, C., Lee, C., Marshall, B., & Wiliam, D. (2003). *Assessment for learning: Putting it into practice.* Buckingham, UK: Open University Press.

Black, P., Harrison, C., Lee, C., Marshall, B., & Wiliam, D. (2004). Working inside the black box: Assessment for learning in the classroom. *Phi Delta Kappan, 86*(1), 8–21.

Black, P., & Wiliam, D. (1998). Inside the black box: Raising standards through classroom assessment. *Phi Delta Kappan, 80*(2), 139–147.

Butler, R. (1988). Enhancing and undermining intrinsic motivation. *British Journal of Educational Psychology, 58*, 1–14.

Davis, B. (1997). Listening for differences: An evolving conception of mathematics teaching. *Journal for Research in Mathematics Education, 28*(3), 355–376.

Wiliam, D. (2005). Keeping learning on track: Formative assessment and the regulation of learning. In M. Coupland, J. Anderson, & T. Spencer (Eds.), *Making mathematics vital: Proceedings of the twentieth biennial conference of the Australian Association of Mathematics Teachers* (pp. 26–40). Adelaide, Australia: Australian Association of Mathematics Teachers.

Wiliam, D., Lee, C., Harrison, C., & Black, P. J. (2004). Teachers developing assessment for learning: Impact on student achievement. *Assessment in Education: Principles, Policy & Practice, 11*(1), 49–65.

Part 2—Multiple Sources of Information Gathering

We have established assessment as the process for collecting information, so it is important to know where and how the information can be gathered in classroom settings. Collecting information about student learning from multiple data points is imperative if a teacher wants a clear picture of where students are in relation to the intended targets. By looking at students through varying lenses, teachers have the opportunity to view student learning in multiple ways and make more valid interpretations of progress or misconceptions. This leads to the appropriate action, whether it is re-teaching, remediation for a small group, individual attention for a specific student, for extension or acceleration of learning.

There are three main sources of classroom data related to student learning—products, observations, and conversations/communications. It is important that classroom assessment practice includes all three sources of student learning data during a unit of study. Different standards and learning targets require students to demonstrate various skills and varying levels of proficiency, and it is only through the effective use of these three sources of data that specific goals may be reached. To effectively use multiple sources of information, teachers need to plan or "engineer" how these data points will be incorporated into a unit of study, how to use the information that is gathered, and how students will receive feedback based on the information. Since formative assessment is a process that occurs during the instructional cycle, it is necessary to use varying forms of information gathering as part of the daily routine. These are not traditional tests, but rather ways of determining what students know at critical points during instruction.

Examples:
Products: journal entries, graphic organizers, quizzes, tests, projects, self-assessments, reports, and homework.
Observation: group work, working with manipulatives, technology use, role-plays, demonstrations, and experiments.
Conversations/communications: teacher conferences, oral presentations, peer conferences, and question-and-answer sessions.

Grade level and content heavily influence a teacher's decision to fully utilize the three sources of student learning data. Most primary teachers are excellent in the use of communication, which is partially attributed to familiarity with their students and contact for an entire day. They also incorporate observation as students in early elementary grades are limited in the types of products they can complete independently. Many secondary teachers use a large number of products because of their content-specific nature, but observation and communication are often neglected. Middle school teachers often create opportunities for students to work collaboratively, but observation of this work is not often used as a means to provide feedback. Teachers generally circulate to respond to needs as they arise or to manage behavior.

One carefully orchestrated activity can yield information on all three student learning data points. Here is an example.

1. Teacher plans for students to use manipulatives to demonstrate a math problem-solving concept.

2. Prior to the activity, the teacher clarifies the learning intention (target) and establishes the criteria for success. In this case, the teacher uses a rubric to help students understand how their performance will be evaluated. The teacher also explains that while students are working, the teacher will circulate and take notes on what he or she observes about the student learning based on the criteria.

3. The students begin the task and the teacher circulates, noting observations. When the teacher stops and asks a student to explain something, this is a communication/conversation.

4. At the end of the activity, the teacher provides whole class communication (feedback) regarding the observations.

5. The teacher asks several students to demonstrate their problem-solving techniques. This is a peer-to-peer communication. The teacher hears how students explain their specific processes and can then provide feedback to the presenting students or elicit feedback from others in the class.

6. The teacher notes which students may need small group or individual attention to clarify misconceptions observed during the activity and the debriefing of solutions at the end.

In this example, an activity using manipulatives (a product based on using materials to assist students with problem solving) creates an opportunity for the teacher to watch students engaged in the activity (observation), and concludes with three points of feedback: individual student, whole class, and peer-to-peer (communications/conversations). The teacher successfully gathered information from all three student learning data points within the duration of one activity.

Given the number of students for which most middle school teachers are responsible, it is necessary to understand that information gathering using multiple sources is not an expectation for every student every day. Teachers can plan the most effective strategy for the lesson and target or single out individual students in need of specific feedback for varying reasons based on previous sources of information. The important thing to remember is that the more opportunity there is to look at students through different lenses, the more focused the teacher will be in understanding all students as learners.

Activity: Products, Observation, and Communication

Directions: Use the following tasks to focus on the importance of using multiple forms of information gathering to make valid instructional decisions.

Task One: Review an upcoming unit of study for assessment opportunities. Determine how and where you could incorporate multiple sources of information gathering. Use the *Multiple Forms of Information Gathering* template to guide your thinking.

Multiple Forms of Information Gathering

Review your classroom practice (instruction and assessment) for one unit of study. Provide examples of how you could incorporate products, observations, and communications/conversations.

1. Types of products you requested:

2. Observations you conducted:

3. Conversations and communications you had with students both individually and in small groups:

4. What conclusions can you draw regarding your sources of information regarding student learning and levels of understanding?

Task Two: Meet with your team and share your findings. Use these questions to guide your discussion:

1. What did this activity reveal about your classroom practices?

2. What could you do to be more effective in the use of various data points?

3. How will this level of information gathering assist you in your instructional process?

4. How will it help students move forward in their learning?

Part 3—The Feedback Loop

Everyone wants and needs feedback on the progress toward any goal. Learning is a trial-and-error process, and feedback keeps the momentum on a clear path to achievement. Adjusting misconceptions, fine-tuning a process, or correcting errors during the learning, whether it is learning a sport or biology, keeps the learner on track for success. One of the most important responsibilities of a classroom teacher is to provide students with information about their strengths and their weaknesses *during* the learning process.

Depending on the learning intention or target, feedback may take different forms. There is both *evaluative* feedback and *descriptive* feedback. Evaluative feedback tells learners how they compare with others or provides a value judgment summarizing the quality of the learning. Examples include the use of grades, percentages, or unexplained comments such as "Good work" or "Try harder." Descriptive feedback is specific information in the form of written comments or conversations that help the learner understand what to do to improve.

Evaluative Feedback	Descriptive Feedback
A- 7/10 Good essay Nice work You've improved. You achieved the target.	This is a well-written draft of your essay. You have covered the main points discussed in your opening paragraph. Now, which point do you think you could elaborate on by providing more information?

Evaluative feedback is the direct result of summative assessment. Inexplicit comments like "Good work" or "Try harder" do not provide students with guidance on how to improve or move to the next step in their learning. Students do not recognize what was good about the work and are left to make assumptions that may or may not be accurate reflections of their learning. Descriptive feedback is a crucial part of formative assessment, and effective classroom assessment requires educators to provide descriptive rather than evaluative feedback to students during the learning process and on formative measures of learning.

Feedback is integral to moving students forward in their learning, and it can be used with any student learning data collection point—products, observations, or communications/conversations. This does not mean that teachers are to include descriptive feedback for every student and for every assignment or task every day. This is not possible in most classrooms. Teachers must look at the big picture and intentionally plan to use descriptive feedback for every student over a period of time.

Specific feedback related to learning targets is necessary, but teachers should keep in mind the length or the complexity of the feedback they provide should be dependent on the needs of individual students. For example, if feedback does not meet the learner's needs or is too long or too complex, a student could choose to ignore it, and the feedback becomes useless (Shute, 2008).

Effective descriptive feedback describes features of work or performance, relates directly to learning targets, points out strengths, and gives specific information about how to improve.

It is best to think of descriptive feedback as a three-part comment.

1. Aspects of the work that are accurate

2. Aspects of the work that need improvement

3. Clues, suggestions, or questions that will guide the student toward improvement without providing the exact correction

A non-negotiable key for descriptive feedback is providing opportunities for the student to use it!

While everyone is in agreement about the value of descriptive feedback, lack of time, number of students, and the number of assignments all can prevent teachers from utilizing this key strategy. Yet the research on its value is very compelling. "Descriptive feedback—specific comments about the quality or characteristics of the work itself—have a positive impact on motivation and learning" (Black & Wiliam, 1998).

Many educators have developed techniques for the purposeful use of descriptive feedback. One of the tasks with your team will be to brainstorm and develop ideas to encourage and incorporate its use as part of formative assessment classroom practice.

Activity: Using Feedback to Provide an Opportunity to Improve

Directions: Use the following tasks to focus on the importance of using descriptive feedback and providing students with the opportunity to improve.

Task One: Review the examples of evaluative and descriptive feedback. What do you use most often in your class? Why? Share with your team.

Task Two: To study the impact of descriptive feedback, use it with your students. Have them complete an ungraded assignment or task and provide them with descriptive feedback based on the target. Students then need the opportunity to complete the assignment or task taking advantages of the comments you provided them. Observe student reactions and discuss this strategy with them. How did it assist them with their learning?

Task Three: Meet with your team and share your findings. Use these questions to guide your discussions:

- What were the advantages of using descriptive feedback?

- How did your students respond?

- Did students demonstrate noticeable changes in their work when given the opportunity to adjust after the feedback?

- Did you encounter any difficulties during the process? Share them with your teammates and brainstorm ways to minimize or eliminate them.

Closing Thoughts
Student Involvement—The Center of Success

The information provided in this book is designed to stimulate reflection on current assessment practices, provide a venue for collegial discussions and investigations, and reveal strategies and methods to link assessment with instruction. Through the professional inquiry process, teachers take initial and risk-free steps to create an opportunity to learn, reflect on, try, and revise instructional practice. Effective classroom assessment practices are not a pedagogy that instantaneously improves. But with time and support from colleagues, assessment will become an integral and motivating source of information for both teachers and students.

When classroom assessment practices are employed at a high level of effectiveness, research indicates student learning improves and a culture of success is achieved. A by-product of using both high-quality summative assessment and formative measures is that students are placed at the center of the learning process. This is especially true with formative assessment. Formative assessment is a classroom process that places students at the center and engages them as owners of their own learning.

"When students are involved in the assessment process, they are required to think about their own learning, articulate what they understand and what they still need to learn—and achievement improves," (Black & Wiliam, 1998).

Each of the modules has provided insights into the value of linking assessment with instruction and the subsequent improvement of student learning. Because students are the only ones who will decide whether or not they are going to learn, teachers must shift their assessment practices to make achievement more attractive or rewarding for students. For students to step up as owners of their learning, they must be engaged, informed, and aware of the integral role they play in their education. The main reason students give for not taking such steps is fear of failure, often based on earlier experiences. Placing students at the center of their own learning and supporting them through the process by presenting a clear picture of the intended goals, establishing a road map on how to achieve the goals, and providing ongoing feedback to reach the goals will guide students to success.

No one wants students to emotionally check out from their education because they have not met success or do not understand what success looks like. The best way to prevent this is to know what students know and make the necessary adjustments to keep students moving forward day-to-day. Assessment is the key to educators' instructional information needs. With intention and purpose, effective classroom assessment practices help to create a classroom environment rich with student involvement and student achievement. We hope this resource has started you on your journey!

Appendix A:
Supplemental Materials

- A Side-by-Side View of Bloom's Taxonomy & Webb's Depth of Knowledge

- Applying Webb's Depth of Knowledge (DOK)

- Applying Bloom's Taxonomy

Cognitive Complexity

A Side-by-Side View of Bloom's Taxonomy & Webb's Depth of Knowledge

Bloom's Taxonomy	Webb's Depth of Knowledge
KNOWLEDGE The recall of specifics and universals, involving little more than brining to mind the appropriate material.	**Level 1** **RECALL** Recall of fact, information, or procedure
	Level 2 **BASIC APPLICATION OF SKILL/ CONCEPT** Use of information, conceptual knowledge, procedures, two or more steps, etc.
COMPREHENSION Ability to process knowledge on a low level such that the knowledge can be reproduced or communicated without verbatim repetition.	
APPLICATION The use of abstractions in concrete situations.	**Level 3** **STRATEGIC THINKING** Requires reasoning, developing a plan or sequence of steps; has some complexity; more than one possible answer. At the classroom level, these tasks generally take up to 10 minutes to complete. This is not a to-the-minute requirement, but rather a guideline.
ANALYSIS "The breakdown of a situation into its component parts."	
SYNTHESIS & EVALUATION Putting together elements and parts to form a whole, and then making value judgments about the method.	**Level 4** **EXTENDED THINKING** Requires investigation; time to think and process multiple conditions of the problem or task. At the classroom level, these non-routine tasks generally take more than 10 minutes to complete. This is not a to-the-minute "requirement," but rather a guideline. A specific time requirement is not a distinguishing factor for LEVEL 4.
EVALUATION Making value judgments about a method, information, ideas, or arguments.	

In classroom application, it is important to understand both Bloom's Taxonomy and Webb's Depth of Knowledge. Their use varies among states. Some states use DOK for state assessment, and some use Bloom's. Knowing which is used and under what circumstances is pertinent information, especially at the instructional level. Also, it is important to understand which is being used to frame both instruction *and* assessment in textbooks used in the classroom.

Wyoming School Health and Physical Education Network (2001). Standards, Assessment, and Beyond. Retrieved May 25, 2006, from http://www.uwyo.edu/wyhpenet0/

Applying Webb's Depth of Knowledge (DOK)

Describe		Explain	Interpret
Level One—Recall Useful Verbs	**Level Two—Skill/Concept Useful Verbs**	**Level Three—Strategic Thinking Useful Verbs**	**Level Four—Extended Thinking Useful Verbs**
arrange, calculate, define, draw, identify, list, label, illustrate, measure, memorize, repeat, name, report, quote, match, use, tabulate, recognize, state, recite, recall	infer, categorize, collect & display, identify patterns, graph, organize, classify, separate, describe cause/effect, estimate, compare, relate, construct, modify, predict, interpret, distinguish, use context clues, make observations, summarize, show	revise, assess, develop a logical argument, apprise, construct, use concepts to solve non-routine problems, critique, compare, explain phenomena in terms of concepts, draw conclusions, investigate, formulate, hypothesize, cite evidence, differentiate	design, connect, synthesize, apply concepts, critique, analyze, create, prove
Level One—Recall Activities	**Level Two—Skill/Concept Activities**	**Level Three—Strategic Thinking Activities**	**Level Four—Extended Thinking Activities**
• Recall elements and details of a story structure, such as sequence of events, character, plot, and setting. • Conduct basic mathematical calculations. • Label locations on a map. • Represent words or diagram a scientific concept or relationship. • Perform routine procedures, e.g., measuring, punctuation. • Describe features of a place or people.	• Identify and summarize the major events in a narrative. • Use context cues to identify the meaning of unfamiliar words. • Solve routine multiple-step problems. • Describe the cause/effect of a particular event. • Identify patterns in events or behavior. • Formulate a routine problem given data and conditions. • Organize, represent, and interpret data.	• Support ideas with details and examples. • Use voice appropriate to purpose and audience. • Identify research questions and design investigations or a scientific problem. • Design a scientific model for a complex situation. • Determine author's purpose and describe how it affects interpretation of a reading selection. • Apply a concept in other contexts.	• Conduct a project that requires specifying a problem, designing and conducting an experiment, analyzing its data, and reporting results or solutions. • Apply mathematical model to illuminate a problem or situation. • Analyze and synthesize information from multiple sources. • Describe and illustrate how common themes are found across texts from different cultures. • Design a mathematical model to inform and solve practical or abstract situation.

Adapted from Webb, Norman L., et. al. (2005). Web alignment tool. Retrieved February 2, 2006, from University of Wisconsin–Madison, Wisconsin Center of Educational Research Web site: <http://www.wcer.wisc.edu/WAT/index.aspx>

Applying Bloom's Taxonomy

	Knowledge	Comprehension	Application	Analysis	Synthesis	Evaluation
Useful Verbs or Action Words	who, what, where, when, why describe define, match, omit, select, what does it mean, which one	state in your own words, classify, judge, infer, show, indicate, translate, explain, represent, what would happen if, indicate	predict, what would the result be, choose the best, and apply, identify results of, tell how much change there would be, tell what could happen	distinguish, what motive is there, what's the relationship between, what ideas justify the conclusion, what persuasive technique, what is the function of	create, make, choose, develop, compose, formulate, design, propose an alternative, how would you test, how else could you	appraise; judge; criticize; defend; what fallacies, consistencies, inconsistencies appear, which is more important, moral, better, logical, valid, appropriate; find the errors; compare
Sample Activities	• Make a list of the main events. • Make a timeline of events. • Make a facts chart. • Write a list of any pieces of information you can remember.	• Illustrate what you think the main idea was. • Make a cartoon strip showing the sequence of events. • Write and perform a play based on the story. • Write a summary report of an event. • Prepare a flow chart to illustrate the sequence of events.	• Construct a model to demonstrate how it will work. • Make a papier-mâché map to include relevant information about an event. • Take a collection of photographs to demonstrate a particular point. • Make up a puzzle game using ideas from the study area. • Write a biography of a person. • Review a work of art: form, color. • Write a textbook about … for others.	• Design a questionnaire to gather information. • Write a commercial to sell a new product. • Conduct an investigation to produce information to support a view. • Make a flow chart to show the critical stages. • Write about your feelings in relation to… • Make up a new language code and write materials using it.	• Invent a machine to do a specific task. • Design a building to house your study. • Create a new product. Give it a name and plan a marketing campaign.	• Prepare a list of criteria to judge —, showing priorities and ratings. • Conduct a debate about an issue of special interest. • Make a booklet about five rules you see as important & convince others. • Form a panel to discuss views. • Prepare a case to present your view about ___.

Appendix B: Resources

The following is a list of materials either citied in the work or used as a reference. We highly recommend that these texts be part of your professional reading on the subject of classroom assessment:

Black, P., & Wiliam, D. (1998). Inside the black box: Raising standards through classroom assessment. *Phi Delta Kappan, 80*(2). Retrieved February 16, 2009, from http://www.pdkintl.org/kappan/kbla9810.htm

Black, P., Harrison, C., Lee, C., Marshall, B., & Wiliam, D. (2003). *Assessment for learning: Putting it into practice.* Berkshire, England: Open University Press.

Black, P., Harrison, C., Lee, C., Marshall, B., & Wiliam, D. (2004). Working inside the black box: Assessment for learning in the classroom. *Phi Delta Kappan, 86*(1), 8–21.

Chappuis, J., and Chappuis, S. (2002). *Understanding school assessment: A parent and community guide to helping students learn.* Portland, OR: Assessment Training Institute.

Council of Chief State School Officers. SCASS Health Education and Assessment Project (HEAP). SCASS Formative Assessment for Students and Teachers (FAST). Retrieved February 16, 2009, from http://www.ccsso.org/projects/SCASS/Projects/Health Education Assessment Project/

Heritage, M. (2007). Formative assessment: What do teachers need to know and do? *Phi Delta Kappan, 89*(2), 140–145.

Leahy, S., Lyon, C., Thompson, M., & Wiliam, D. (2005). Classroom assessment: Minute by minute, day by day. *Educational Leadership, 63*(3), 19–24.

National Middle School Association (2006). Research summary: *Characteristics of exemplary schools of young adolescents.* Retrieved February 2, 2009, from http://www.nmsa.org/Research/ResearchSummaries/ExemplarySchools/tabid/256/Default.aspx

Putman, R. T., & Borko, H. (2000). What do new views of knowledge and thinking have to say about research on teacher learning? *Educational Researcher, 29*(1), 4–15.

Sadler, R. (1999). Formative assessment and the design of instructional systems. *Instructional Science, 18*, 119–144.

Shepard, L. (2005). Linking formative assessment to scaffolding. *Educational Leadership, 63*(3), 66–70.

Shute, V. (2008). Focus on formative assessment. Review of Educational Research, 78(153), 1–68.

Stiggins, R. (2004). New assessment beliefs for a new school mission. *Phi Delta Kappan, 86*(1), 22–27.

Stiggins. R., & Chappuis, J. (2006). What a difference a word makes: Assessment FOR learning rather than assessment OF learning helps students succeed. *Journal of Staff Development, 27*(1), 22–27.

Stiggins, R., Arter, J., Chappuis, J., & Chappuis, S. (2006). *Classroom assessment for student learning: Doing it right –using it well.* Portland, OR: ETS Assessment Training Institute.

Appendix C:
Glossary of Assessment Terms

Assessment
The process of gathering information about student achievement, most often in relation to defined learning expectations.

Assessment Literacy
The set of knowledge and skills educators need to gather accurate and reliable information about student learning and to be able to use that information in productive ways.

Assessment Methods
The different ways schools use to evaluate learning. There are four basic categories of assessment methods: selected response, writing assignment, performance, and personal communication.

Benchmarks
Statements of what students should know and do by certain grade levels or times during the school year.

Bias
A lack of objectivity or fairness; used to describe a potential problem in student assessment.

Constructed Response
Free-response or open-ended question with more than one correct answer possible; uses a rubric or scoring guide.

Content Standards

The broadest, most general form of learning expectation from which more specific grade-level curriculum is derived. Content standards describe what a student should know and be able to do.

Curriculum

A more specific version of the standards arranged in a scope and sequence of specific content, usually designed for each subject area at an individual grade level. Curriculum forms the guide for what is to be taught and when.

Descriptive Feedback

Information related to the assigned learning task and provided to students to help them take the next steps in their learning by showing them what they already do well, what they need to do to improve, and how.

Evaluation

The process of collecting information from multiple sources to make judgments, for example, to assign a grade about how well students have learned.

Evaluative Feedback

Feedback that tells learners how they compare with others or that provides a judgment summarizing the quality of the learning. Letter grades, numbers, symbols, and written phrases are typically used to deliver this type of feedback.

Formative Assessment

Formative Assessment is part of the instructional process. When incorporated into classroom practice, it provides the information needed to adjust teaching and learning while they are happening. In this sense, formative assessment informs both teachers and students about student understanding at a point when timely adjustments can be made.

Large-Scale Assessment

Assessments in which large numbers of students participate and from which system-wide (district or state data) are collected. This data is often used for accountability purposes.

Learning Targets

The most specific forms of learning expectations on the path to mastery of a standard or essential question. They define the objectives of lessons, create paths for instruction, form the bases of both formative and summative assessments, and guide descriptive feedback.

Open-Response Tasks

Kind of performance required of students when they are required to generate an answer, rather than to select from among several possible answers.

Performance Assessment

An assessment that requires a student to construct a response, create a product, or perform a demonstration. Evaluation of the knowledge and skills displayed is based on observation and judgment with the help of scoring criteria.

Performance Tasks

The assignment in a performance assessment.

Performance Level or Standard (also known as grade level expectations)
The predetermined level of acceptable performance on an assessment of a standard; answers the question, "How good is good enough?"

Personal Communication
An assessment method in which the teacher asks a question or engages in a dialogue with the student and listens to determine the quality of the response and level of understanding.

Portfolio
A collection of student work that reflects student progress toward the intended learning.

Rubric
A scoring tool or set of criteria used to evaluate student performance on a task or test. Rubrics may be holistic (evaluating the "whole" of the student work) or analytical (evaluating the student work by various categories to determine proficiency).

Scoring Guide
A scoring tool or set of criteria that is unique to the student performance or test item.

Self-Assessment
A process in which students collect information about their own learning, analyze what it reveals about their progress toward the intended learning goals, and plan the next steps in their learning.

Selected-Response Tests
Tests used to measure students' knowledge and reasoning proficiencies. They have one correct answer or a limited number of correct answers and can include multiple-choice, matching, fill-in-the-blank or short answer, and true-false items.

Student-involved Conference
Communication about student learning in which the student takes an active role in planning and delivering the information with the help of the teacher.

Summative Assessment
Summative assessments are given periodically to determine at a particular point in time what students know and do not know. Many associate summative assessments only with standardized tests such as state assessments, but they are also used in and are an important part of district and classroom programs. Summative assessment at the classroom level is used for accountability as part of the grading process.

Multiple Sources of Information Gathering (Triangulation)
The process of collecting information regarding student learning from various data points, e.g. products, observations, communications/conversations.

National Middle School Association

Since 1973, National Middle School Association (NMSA) has been the voice for those committed to the education and well-being of young adolescents and is the only national association dedicated exclusively to middle level youth.

NMSA's members are principals, teachers, central office personnel, professors, college students, parents, community leaders, and educational consultants in the United States, Canada, and 46 other countries. A major advocacy effort is Month of the Young Adolescent. This October celebration engages a wide range of organizations to help schools, families, and communities celebrate and honor young adolescents for their contributions to society.

NMSA offers publications, professional development services, and events for middle level educators seeking to improve the education and overall development of 10- to 15-year-olds. In addition to the highly acclaimed Middle School Journal, Middle Ground magazine, and Research in Middle Level Education Online, we publish more than 100 books on every facet of middle level education. Our landmark position paper, This We Believe, is recognized as the premier statement outlining the vision of middle level education.

Membership is open to anyone committed to the education of young adolescents. Visit www.nmsa.org or call 1-800-528-NMSA for more information.

About the Authors

Author:

Catherine Garrison, M.Ed., is manager of products and services for professional development with Measured Progress. Ms. Garrison works closely with clients and partner organizations to grow and enhance business opportunities as well as develop and present trainings on the topic of classroom assessment. Ms Garrison was an educator for 21 years, teaching high school and middle school English language arts, including sheltered instruction for English language learners. Ms. Garrison also worked as a national language arts consultant and has authored several articles and ancillary materials for textbooks.

Contributing Author

Dennis Chandler, M.Ed., is professional development specialist with Measured Progress. Mr. Chandler collaboratively develops and delivers professional development services related to effective assessment practices to states, districts and schools. Prior to his work with Measured Progress, Mr. Chandler was an educator for more than 30 years, 20 of those years as a classroom teacher.

Contributing Author

Michael Ehringhaus, Ph.D., is director of professional development at Measured Progress and has been involved in the field of education for 40 years. Prior to coming to Measured Progress, Dr. Ehringhaus worked on a wide range of research and test development related to large-scale assessment. Dr. Ehringhaus has also taught multiple subjects and ages ranging from middle school through adult learning in diverse locations from New Zealand to Alaska. Dr. Ehringhaus has been also published widely.

Measured Progress

For 25 years, Measured Progress, a not-for-profit organization, has been committed to supporting educational progress through assessment programs that are closely integrated with curriculum and instruction. The organization partners with states, school districts, and like-minded organizations to provide professional development, assessment, and educational tools that accurately measure student achievement and improve instruction.

Breinigsville, PA USA
18 January 2010
230902BV00003B/1/P